This large crucifix was carved in Chipili, Zambia

*It was given to our Somerset parish in 1995
where it hangs in St Augustine's Church*

The cover picture looks to the Drakensbergs from Natal (once part of Shaka's 'empire')

*Lesotho, known as 'The Kingdom in the Sky', lies to the west of this escarpment
whereas Malawi, termed 'The Warm Heart of Africa', is much further north*

Copyright 2019 Rodney Schofield

All rights reserved. No part of this publication may be reproduced, stored in a retrieval system, or transmitted in any from or by any means, electronic, mechanical, photocopying, recording or otherwise without prior permission from the publishers.

Published by
Luviri Press
P/Bag 201 Luwinga
Mzuzu 2
Malawi

ISBN 978-99960-66-28-3
e ISBN 978-99960-66-29-0

Luviri Press is represented outside Africa by:
African Books Collective Oxford (order@africanbookscollective.com)

www.mzunipress.blogspot.com
www.africanbookscollective.com

Sursum Corda
Celebrating seven years in Africa

Rodney Schofield

African publications
by Rodney Schofield

Jubilee Reflections
    Rich and poor in Christian Perspective
        (Kachere Series, Malawi 2001)

Mystery or Magic
    Biblical replies to the heterodox
        (Kachere Series, Malawi 2004)

Malawi Mailings
    Reflections on missionary life 2000-2003
        (Mzuni Press, Malawi 2014)

Emerging Scriptures
    Torah, Gospel and Qur'an in Christian perspective
        (Mzuni Press, Malawi 2015)

Issues of War
    Christian thinking for the 21st century
        (Luviri Press, Malawi 2018)

Jesus – the Man for others
        (Luviri Press, Malawi 2018)

Contents

"I'm an African too"
Page 1

Lift up your hearts
Page 14

Vocation
Page 20

We lift them to the Lord
Page 32

Inculturation
Page 38

Let us give thanks to the Lord our God
Page 60

Globalisation
Page 66

It is right and just
Page 78

"Small is beautiful"
Page 84

Acknowledgements

This volume is dedicated to Klaus Fiedler, who has been very supportive of my literary efforts over the past twenty years. He encouraged me, while still in Malawi, to pursue a doctorate, and has published several of my books.

Thanks go also to friends and colleagues in both Roma (Lesotho) and Zomba (Malawi) for a range of ideas and information.

Apart from the photographs that appear here, most of the drawings and sketches are by my wife Sarah – with just a few by our children Gabriel and Patricia when they were with us in Lesotho.

I must pay tribute as well to the divinity master who taught me at St Albans School when I was 13 years old. Peter Burton, the Abbey organist, led us through the minor prophets; his favourite verse in the Bible, so he told us, was Amos 4.13 (featured here on page 36). It has ever since continued to inspire me, as it did him. He died tragically that same year – drowning in the school's swimming pool in an attempt to rescue one of his choristers.

"I'm an African too"

In 1983 I responded to a plea from the bishop of Lesotho, on a rare visit to England, to go out to his country (about the size of Wales) as Warden of the Anglican seminary, Lelapa la Jesu (*'the little house of Jesus'*) – well-situated on the campus of the National University of Lesotho at Roma, where I was also to lecture in New Testament Studies. Sarah was very supportive, recalling how her own parents had spent the early years of their marriage in Zaria (Northern Nigeria). Ben was there to train pharmacists, while Pat was a physiotherapist in the nearby mission hospital: this experience in the early 1930s had been very rewarding.

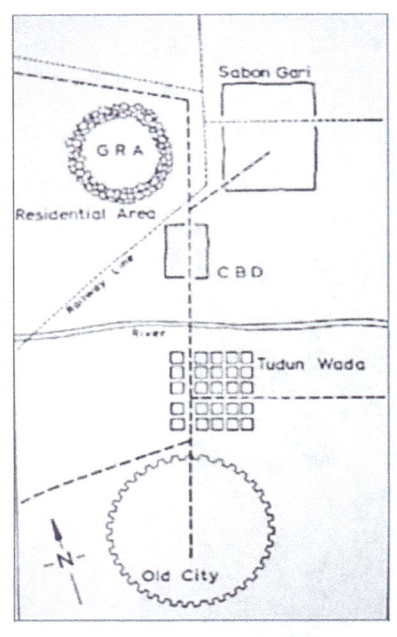

GRA Government Reserve Area

European Residential Area, a separate zone so that native diseases might be caught less easily. At its centre were the Club and its racecourse. It was laid out with avenues of *madaci* and *neem* trees. In the early 1930s there were probably around 150 people living here. There was also an army camp (and a prison). The 'African' hospital, with its pharmacy training school where Ben and Pat lived, was to the south of Zaria.

CBD Central Business District

Sabon Gari or "strangers' quarters" to provide for those working in local commerce or on the railway, some of whom might be southerners (and perhaps Christian): these would come under Residency supervision. However, local Muslims also moved here to take advantage of new business opportunities.

Tudun Wada for Muslim outsiders, laid out on a grid pattern according to government regulations: these were answerable to the Emir.

Old City was the ancient walled town: here Muslims would be free of contaminating European practices (especially the consumption of alcohol) & their (often nominal!) Christian religion. These walls have now largely vanished.

St Bartholomew's, Wusasa (1929), along with the mission school and hospital, was two miles west of Zaria. In 1932, the hospital cared for 441 in-patients – and thousands of out-patients. The church was restored in 2006. Ben played the organ here. After leavng Zaria, he entered ordination training, much influenced by his friend Guy Bullen, by then a bishop in Sudan.

Keeping the peace: a plan of Zaria's different zones in the 1930s

Fifty years later (in the 1980s) it was a time of considerable political unrest across the world. In Europe there were divisions between Bosnians, Serbs and Croatians which would lead eventually to civil war and the end of Yugoslavia as a political entity. In the United States the civil rights campaign continued to grow. In South Africa the anti-apartheid movement went from strength to strength during the 1980s, with white domination ending soon afterwards: Nelson Mandela was released after 27 years in prison and was elected President in 1994. And Lesotho's own government, threatened by an exiled opposition and ill at ease with its nearest neighbour South Africa (which entirely surrounded it, and controlled the flow of traffic in and out of its territory), took the drastic step of seeking help from communist North Korea.

As a family we were not plunged into this tense and unfamiliar scenario without due preparation. We spent a term living together at the College of the Ascension in Birmingham alongside Christians from different churches across the world, including a number of Africans who were studying courses that would enhance their ministry on returning home. The outstanding lecturer whom we came to know quite well was Patrick Kalilombe, formerly the Catholic bishop of Lilongwe in Malawi, but exiled by President Kamuzu Banda because of his encouragement of 'small parish groups': these enabled lay people to exchange ideas and support each other in their perceived Christian callings – a potential threat to any dictator, which was what Banda had now become. Although our lectures and tutorials focused more on cultural and practical matters (including linguistics), we also discussed a little of the current political questions, including what might happen within apartheid-riven South Africa, soon to be our new neighbour.

The broader issue was then – and still remains – that of 'multiculturalism'. This is inevitably more problematic in urban areas, where different ethnic or religious communities live close together and can scarcely ignore their diverse practices and beliefs. Even a mainly secular society which promotes tolerance and respect for different lifestyles has its limits, and tends to legislate against extremist behaviour. Yet, in turn, mainstream Christians and Muslims are distinctly uncomfortable with those liberal ('individualistic') cultures in which activities such as pornography and drug taking are largely unregulated and their social consequences ignored. Given too that factional strife is far from unknown within a supposedly single creed, it would be idealistic to imagine that mutual forbearance can always be achieved: tribalism is never very far away, and assumes many different guises in the modern world. This does not mean that the goal of multiculturalism must necessarily be abandoned, but rather that there must be patience and flexibility in the political means by which it can be reached – and subsequently maintained.

A weakness of our time in Birmingham was however a limitation on discussion and debate. Indeed, one of the questions I raised in a tutorial session about the political process to end apartheid in South Africa was deemed sufficiently improper that my missionary appointment was put on hold. Observing that the tribal homelands were distinctly under-resourced, I had wondered whether their economic revival along with improved geographic coherence – and perhaps greater independence – might not enhance several of the non-white populations. This single question (*sic*) was held by the college staff to be clear evidence that I had no respect for Africans! All travel arrangements were then suspended until a staff member came from London to resolve matters. Subsequently, when visiting Transkei from Lesotho, I discovered that my question was actually a live issue for the Xhosa people who lived there – not entirely dissimilar to the debate promoted by Scottish or Welsh nationalists advocating a better future outside the United Kingdom.

Political meetings were very restricted in Lesotho itself soon after we arrived there. Any deliberations involving more than three people were banned by the government, and although I encouraged our students to think through both the personal and public implications of their Christian faith most of them were reluctant to do so in class – in case one of their colleagues reported adversely to the ruling authority (or its minions). In other words, there was quite an atmosphere of intimidation and fear. On one occasion I ventured some criticism of the government in a sermon and was warned by a member of the congregation afterwards to be careful or I would face deportation.

There was, however, one slogan which united our students: 'Africa for the Africans'. After centuries of colonial exploitation this signals to the rest of the world that Africans deserve to be fully respected as people, and that their lands and resources are not there simply for the taking: a message which certainly had my support. Our students were glad to hear this, but were puzzled when I added 'and I'm an African too – at least in my ancestry'. So I explained how important it is to remember that from the dawn of human history most tribes have sooner or later been on the move, sometimes driven by war but more often seeking new pastures or perhaps better trading opportunities. The Basotho people themselves fled westwards in the early 19th century from the brutal Zulu campaigns led by king Shaka, until at last they reached their present territory (better protected by the Drakensberg range of mountains). Other neighbouring tribes were scattered also – yet in earlier centuries many of them had in any case originated much further north in Africa. Europeans and Asians can likewise trace their distant ancestry to Africa, most likely to its eastern Rift Valley, and migration continues as much today as it has always done in the past. None of us can claim the land where we live now as our exclusive inheritance: DNA testing can often surprise those who imagine otherwise!

There was also an uncomfortable aspect of the slogan 'Africa for the Africans' which needed to be faced more honestly. Before we had been very long at the seminary I went to visit Bishop Desmond Tutu in Johannesburg about the possibility of some of his ordinands studying with us (rather than elsewhere). The underlying objective was to bind us more closely to the province of Southern Africa than had recently been possible – following a decision of the South African government to exclude Basotho and Swazi students from their colleges, thus imposing a degree of apartheid on the churches' programme of priestly formation. Bishop Tutu, who had once taught in Roma, willingly acceded to the request, enabling a number of men from Soweto soon to join us at Lelapa la Jesu. Their background was very different from the mainly rural experience of our existing students, so it was not surprising that there were sometimes disagreements between them. What we had not expected were the occasional tensions that flared up amongst our newcomers, which – so they reported – were nothing compared to the inter-tribal feuding from which they had emerged back in Soweto. If 'Africans' ever took control of their country, one began to wonder, how would power and influence be shared between the various tribal groupings? Indeed, would a change of government ever enable those at the bottom of the pile to be any better off at all than under the present (white) regime?

A decade and more later, when we returned to Africa, precisely the same questions arose in Malawi, which by then had been independent and self-governing for nearly forty years. There had certainly been a new constitution and several 'democratic' elections since Banda's deposition, but the numerical strength of the different tribal groupings in the country was the main determining factor in any vote. When a general election was announced during our time there, I recall asking what each of the political parties stood for – had they published any manifestos, for example. The question was met with blank astonishment: 'we just back the man from our own tribe' was the usual response, quite regardless of any particular policies he may have espoused. In fact, of course, voters knew that whoever won the election would reward their own kind and as far as possible would attempt to starve the opposition into the ground. This was to teach people a lesson: one politician actually said, 'Your constituency returned the wrong man (or woman), so don't expect much in the way of new roads, bridges, schools, clinics etc'.

It would nevertheless be naïve not to admit that even those who had voted the government into power would not gain very much from it. African culture once espoused an ethic in which communities pooled their blessings: thus, if a person's luck changed for the better his family – perhaps his whole village – could expect to share it. So it was sad to see how much wealth was corruptly accumulated to their private use by government ministers, by civil servants, or by some of those involved with NGOs. After leaving Malawi we heard from friends who remained in the country of their growing sadness, if not despair, at the continually deteriorating scenario.

For the most part our students saw themselves at the service of others through their ministry in the Church – although undoubtedly there were times when they regarded the institutional Church as a well-heeled global organisation able to provide better living conditions and job prospects than those they might otherwise expect. Thus, in Lesotho one of our students Musa, who frequently absented himself from the seminary, admitted that he had sought admission only after hearing his father's advice that Anglican priests were paid a pension on their retirement, whereas school teachers were not. Occasionally too (as no doubt happens in most colleges) some students complained that they were inadequately fed – why was a meat dish not being provided *twice* every day, as was their right? Only one seminarian in Roma, however, ever aligned himself with a 'black power' group; this was Dominic from Swaziland, who kept a poster in his room which displayed a clenched fist. He also regarded Africans of other tribes as 'unclean', and demanded a new bottle of Dettol each week to contain their contamination: in the end, he had to be asked to pack his bags.

In Malawi there were fewer problematic students, although from time to time one of those graduating would disappear from the ranks of the clergy. Having secured a diploma or degree at the church's expense he would then apply for a better-paid job in commerce or as a civil servant. Roy's ambitions were a little different: on being appointed to a parish he demanded to be given a motor car 'as undoubtedly would be done' were he in England. Although this attitude was exceptional within the college, it sadly took root among many of the clergy of the Lake diocese during – and more significantly after – our time in Malawi. Tensions mounted when the need arose to appoint a new diocesan bishop: the obvious choice was between a couple of experienced African priests, but a vociferous minority lobbied hard for an expatriate priest from London, who hardly knew Malawi at all but had *supplied funding* from his parish and was therefore seen as a potential 'magic money tree' capable of increasing clergy stipends. Physical violence was used, even within church buildings; but worst of all was when a long-standing missionary Rodney Hunter, who stood firmly in favour of an African bishop, was murdered in his bed.

Going out to Africa as a missionary might begin to sound a hazardous enterprise! I am reminded though of a book written by one of our friends in Malawi (Stephen Carr) about his life as a missionary farmer in several African countries: it bears the title *Surprised by Joy.* Despite their deprivations and difficulties (poverty, lack of educational or health facilities, floods, droughts, political oppression, civil war, to name but a few) many Africans have a remarkable resilience that enables them to live life to the full, to celebrate in song and dance, to be amazingly hospitable, and to foster a community spirit (not always so evident now in the West). So, although we went out to share some of our own benefits and experiences, we also learnt much from our hosts and will ever be grateful to them: hence the title of this book *Sursum Corda* ('Lift up your hearts'). In fact, our missionary society (USPG) came to describe our role as that of 'partnering' the local churches.

After spending three years in Lesotho, we returned to England still hoping to serve once again in Africa. The opportunity presented itself in 1999 to teach at Zomba Theological College in Malawi, and this time we were able to remain there for four years. Those seven years were certainly the most fulfilling years of my priestly ministry – and part of us both still 'remains' in Africa: there are the people we helped who now have fruitful occupations; there are churches (and a theological college) whose construction we assisted; while more recently there have been consignments of books sent out to help fill the library shelves of seminaries, as well as some half dozen books written primarily for African students – and published on their own continent.

Carolyn Pickson (L) in her secretarial office in Zomba (R) in her own home in 2008

Carolyn's parents had both died of AIDS: she lived with us for 4 years, first completing her school certificate before gaining secretarial qualifications. After a post with TEEM, she moved to be a secretary at Chancellor College. Her income helps to support her extended family, who live next door to where we helped her build her own home.

Andy Banda (L) by Rodney Hunter's grave in Nkhotakota (R) on his ordination day

Initially a potter in Nkhotakota (where we met him in 2001 and heard of his conversion from Islam and his aspiration to be a Christian priest), Andy was helped through his school certificate, then gained a degree at Mzuzu University, and after overcoming many difficulties was ordained in 2016 for the Anglican diocese of Northern Malawi. We sent him a set of white vestments when he moved to a poor 'mission' parish on the border with Zambia.

St Andrew's Chapel, Lelapa la Jesu, Roma

Built in 1985-6, the structure is supported by laminated half portals – so the walls are not load-bearing, enabling the chapel to be extended if necessary – as happened in 2010.

Leonard Kamungu Theological College, Zomba

The site had been owned by the Anglican Church of Malawi for some years, but was leased to the company constructing Zomba's new dam. When their project was completed in 2002, the buildings reverted to ACM, but needed considerable adaptation for use as a college. Funding was generously provided by St John's College, Cambridge. Sarah spent many hours with Kidman establishing the gardens here. The pictures above were taken in 2008 on a brief visit.

As regards the availability of books, it was soon evident at Lelapa la Jesu that the seminary library had been long neglected, but also apparent that there were few bookshops worthy of the name anywhere in Lesotho – other than perhaps an evangelical store in Morija. The same was true in Malawi, as I noted in 2000:

> Nowhere [here] is there any bookshop where academic or even fairly serious books can be obtained. Times Bookshops are represented in the larger towns, but sell only stationery, newspapers and a limited range of popular fiction. The churches set up a few bookshops of their own, but – apart from the one attached to the Catholic church in Balaka, home of the Montfort Press – these are stocked entirely with rather tired 1950s and 1960s devotional tracts of a broadly evangelical persuasion, many of which have been donated by ministers in England on reaching their retirement. Under Dr Banda's regime the Malawi Book Service flourished and sold good non-fiction and academic works, but only because of its monopoly on the sale of school textbooks. After the 1994 elections this monopoly ended and with it the MBS itself ... Can you begin to imagine what it is like to live in a country where there are virtually no books or only a few (possibly outdated) second-hand ones?
>
> This situation affects our teaching in more than one way. Where there is only one available book on a given subject, it is treated with undue reverence. My classes are constantly rather shocked when I suggest that the author may have got it wrong, and that they should use their own critical faculties. In biblical studies in particular I emphasise that the conclusion is only as strong as the evidence supporting it, so students should not treat their commentaries as final dogmatic authorities. But it is not easy for any society that has been under totalitarian rule for 30 years, as was Malawi under Dr Banda, to learn to debate and to discuss freely and to weigh the strength of different arguments.

Fortunately in Malawi itself the religious studies department at the university had not long since set up its own publishing arm, the Kachere Press, whose office was conveniently on our college campus. In 2001 they published the first of my offerings, *Jubilee Reflections*, whose research was derived as much as possible from internet sources as a way of demonstrating to our students what might still be achieved even without a rich resource of books. It followed on the widespread (partial) cancellation of Third World debt in the millennial year 2000, both by examining how Malawi's overseas debts had escalated and by looking back at developing Christian attitudes to wealth, borrowing and lending, and related issues. The next book, *Mystery or Magic*, discussed the hugely topical problem of African witchcraft, very much still alive in Malawi.

Back in England the regular monthly reports that I had circulated to friends and parishes during those four years in Central Africa were collected together under the title *Malawi Mailings*; these reflected upon the various challenges that confronted both our college and the churches generally, and aimed to help people back home appreciate the very different living conditions that most Malawians face. It was published once more by Klaus Fiedler, now at Mzuzu University running a similar set-up known as the Mzuni Press. A further title was added soon afterwards, *Emerging Scriptures*, which looked at the history of those Jewish and Christian writings that came to be given 'canonical' status, but also surveyed the emergence of the Qur'an – noting its partial reliance upon biblical and apocryphal sources and observing its promulgation and impact in the centuries that followed. (I was heartened by the recent landmark meeting between Pope Francis and the Grand Imam of al-Azhar and their joint statement, 'The pluralism and the diversity of religions … are willed by God in his wisdom' – which must surely help to ease religious tensions in the world.)

More recently the Luviri Press has taken over from Mzuni, and in 2018 published both *Issues of War* (summarising the development of Christian teaching over the years) and *Jesus – the Man for others*, which is intended to focus all the previous writings on the one central truth of our Christian faith, the person, the life, mission and teaching of Christ himself.

Lift up your hearts

The heavens are telling the glory of God;
and the firmament proclaims his handiwork.

Day to day pours forth speech,
and night to night declares knowledge.
There is no speech, nor are there words;
their voice is not heard;
yet their voice goes out through all the earth,
and their words to the end of the world.
In them he has set a tent for the sun,
(*Psalm 19.1-4*)

Above **Purple-crested lourie**

Below **Black-eyed bulbul**

Seen in our garden in Malawi

Thou visitest the earth and waterest it,
thou greatly enrichest it;
the river of God is full of water;
thou providest their grain,
for so thou hast prepared it.
Thou waterest its furrows abundantly,
settling its ridges,
softening it with showers,
and blessing its growth.
Thou crownest the year with thy bounty;
the tracks of thy chariot drip with fatness.
The pastures of the wilderness drip,
the hills gird themselves with joy,
the meadows clothe themselves with flocks,
the valleys deck themselves with grain,
they shout and sing together for joy.
(Psalm 65.9-13)

Above **Green woodpecker**

Below **Red bishop-bird**
often seen in Lesotho

Phahamisang lipelo tsa lona

Let the mountains bear prosperity for the people,
and the hills, in righteousness!
May he defend the cause of the poor of the people,
give deliverance to the needy,
and crush the oppressor!
May he live while the sun endures,
and as long as the moon, throughout all generations!
May he be like rain that falls on the mown grass,
like showers that water the earth!
In his days may righteousness flourish,
and peace abound, till the moon be no more!
(*Psalm 72.3-7*)

Lesotho abounds in butterflies
also featured on postage stamps

Praise the Lord!
For it is good to sing praises to our God;
for he is gracious, and a song of praise is seemly.
The Lord builds up Jerusalem;
he gathers the outcasts of Israel.
He heals the brokenhearted,
and binds up their wounds.
He determines the number of the stars,
he gives to all of them their names.
Great is our Lord, and abundant in power;
his understanding is beyond measure.
The Lord lifts up the downtrodden,
he casts the wicked to the ground.
Sing to the Lord with thanksgiving;
make melody to our God upon the lyre!
He covers the heavens with clouds,
he prepares rain for the earth,
he makes grass grow upon the hills.
He gives to the beasts their food,
and to the young ravens which cry.
(*Psalm 147.1-9*)

Left Pied kingfisher

Right Pel's fishing owl *in Malawi*

Bottom right Aloes *on a Lesotho tapestry*

Kwezani mitima yanu

Praise the Lord from the earth,
you sea monsters and all deeps,
fire and hail, snow and frost,
stormy wind fulfilling his command!
Mountains and all hills,
fruit trees and all cedars!
Beasts and all cattle,
creeping things and flying birds!
Kings of the earth and all peoples,
princes and all rulers of the earth!
Young men and maidens together,
old men and children!
Let them praise the name of the Lord,
for his name alone is exalted;
his glory is above earth and heaven.
He has raised up a horn for his people,
praise for all his saints,
for the people of Israel who are near to him.
(*Psalm 148.7-14*)

***Above left* Jacana**

***Above* Wooden crane**

***Left* Hoopoe**

From Malawi

Then the Lord God formed man of dust from the ground, and breathed into his nostrils the breath of life; and man became a living being.
And the Lord God planted a garden in Eden, in the east; and there he put the man whom he had formed.
And out of the ground the Lord God made to grow every tree that is pleasant to the sight and good for food, the tree of life also in the midst of the garden, and the tree of the knowledge of good and evil.
(*Genesis 2.7-9*)

View of Mulanje mountain from our garden in Zomba

Vocation

The scene pictured above shows a young herd boy on a mountain side in Lesotho. He would probably tend the family's sheep and goats here each summer, alongside others of a similar age. They would be supplied with sacks of maize to cook over open fires as their staple food, sheltering when necessary in simple huts. Their diet would be supplemented by mice and small birds, often shot down with catapults. The situation in Malawi was a little different, as herding was far less common: nevertheless, as harvest time approached, children would be sent into the fields each day to keep the crops from being raided by birds or rodents – hence school attendances might then go temporarily into decline. These practices would not affect urban populations nearly so much, but do indicate how hard it might be for some children to progress educationally and to be equipped for life in a fast-changing world. The choices open to them on reaching adulthood would be somewhat limited.

In Western societies, by contrast, even those growing up in deprived areas have a much wider range of opportunities they could pursue, given the necessary support and determination. Yet they might still be relatively deficient in some areas of life compared with the above-mentioned African children, simply because the latter have far more exposure to the natural world, which can allow its wonder and mystery to work upon the imagination, resulting – quite often perhaps? – in a deeper spiritual awareness than might be gained from (say) an addiction to computer games or to social media. When youngsters in the West look up to the stars, do they simply recall science fiction accounts of alien activity, or do they ponder the origin of this vast universe? When they climb a mountain, is it simply to boost their physical prowess, or does it provide them with the space and time for contemplating their past, present and future lives? Or again, if one is surrounded by an amazing variety of vegetation, is it not likely that its beauty and intricacy will foster a more measured 'ecological' respect than is found among either the litter louts who increasingly despoil our environment or the human predators who raid it solely to enrich themselves?

Surveys in Western countries now suggest that there are growing numbers of people who describe themselves as having 'no religion'. Globally this bucks the trend, which sees (for example) Christian churches continuing to swell their ranks worldwide while Islam in its different manifestations is predicted to have the most numerous followers by the end of the twenty-first century. It is certainly clear that in England both Catholic and Anglican churches are on the wane, and are struggling to find enough clergy – vocations having fallen off in the past twenty years. Whereas the Church of England has alleviated the situation by recruiting older people (of both genders) to be 'non-stipendiary' ministers, the Catholic Church has come to rely much more upon priests from overseas (Poland, Kerala, Nigeria spring particularly to mind) – and indeed the arrival of devout immigrants from abroad has also slowed the decline in congregational attendance. Even though there is no simple way to significantly boost the number of priestly vocations without addressing the wider challenge of the Church's mission to the population generally – the proportion of 'the faithful' who hear God's call to ordained ministry is unlikely to vary hugely – it is nevertheless worthwhile exploring what factors may sometimes have been vocationally significant.

As John Henry Newman was always ready to emphasise, 'People are variously constituted; what influences one does not influence another' – or again, 'The medicines necessary for our souls are very different from each other. Thus God leads us by strange ways'. In his *Essay in Aid of a Grammar of Assent* (1870) he did, however, point to an openness of heart and mind (an 'antecedent expectancy') as a precondition for discovering one's vocation. This arguably includes an awareness of God's mysterious presence within the created order, or – in African terms – a spiritual sensitivity. There are a host of possible stimuli:

> The heart is commonly reached, not through the reason, but through the imagination, by means of direct impressions, by the testimony of facts and events, by history, by description. Persons influence us, voices melt us, looks subdue us, deeds inflame us.

Yet, although Newman insisted that God's calling is distinctly personal (echoing St Paul's advice to Christians at Corinth), he admitted that not all will easily realise it for themselves:

> God has created me to do Him some definite service. He has committed some work to me which He has not committed to another. I have my mission. I may never know it in this life, but I shall be told it in the next. I am a link in a chain, a bond of connection between persons. He has not created me for naught. I shall do good; I shall do His work. I shall be an angel of peace, a preacher of truth in my own place, while not intending it if I do but keep His commandments.

No single vocational path is likely to be the same for all. Sometimes a number of wrong choices need to be explored first, and it is only when they seem to be unfruitful that a better way forward can emerge. Before outlining the background to my own (missionary) calling, the very different circumstances faced by our Malawi protégés Andy and Carolyn (as seen in the photographs shown earlier) are worth mentioning.

On our first meeting with him in Nkhotakota, Andrew explained that he had been brought up in a strongly Muslim household. His father was effectively the local sheikh, and had taken advantage of his position to work his way through a considerable number of wives. The Qur'an limits these to a maximum of four – and even then insists that they should all be treated 'equally', which it points out is a challenging ideal unlikely very often to be realised. Andy's father made a point of divorcing many of his wives in order to acquire new ones, a vicious habit which in the end disturbed Andy so much that he broke away from his home and was given refuge by neighbouring Christians. However, he still suffered periodic attacks and beatings from his father and his brothers, which served only to reinforce his growing Christian convictions. It was in 2001 that he confessed his longing to be ordained as a Christian priest. I pointed out there was a long road to travel, especially as he had few educational qualifications. Fortunately, a fellow missionary of much experience who had taught in seminaries, Canon Rodney Hunter, was resident not far away, and readily took Andy under his wing. He gained his Malawi school certificate, then studied at Mzuzu University; but by now problems had arisen because of bitter feuding (outlined earlier) within the local Anglican diocese regarding the appointment of a new bishop. Rodney Hunter believed firmly that an African would best meet needs of the diocese, and would maintain the traditions of pastoral care and clear teaching that had been inculcated for many years by UMCA (the Universities Mission to Central Africa – later absorbed into USPG). Others, however, sought an expatriate, in the hope that this would bring money into the diocese from abroad. When Rodney was murdered, it was Andy who raised the funds for his headstone – in consequence of which he too became a target for persecution and was certainly much delayed in progressing towards his goal of ministry. For a time his energy went into a school to the south of Nkhotakota, not far from the pottery where he had once worked. He also pondered whether – after being physically chased out of an Anglican church service – he should explore ordination in the Catholic Church, but decided otherwise on realising that this also required a commitment to celibacy, which was not his particular calling. Providentially, through the help of a former bishop of Northern Malawi (Jack Biggars, an American Episcopalian who retained his links with the country), Andy was then steered away from the still seething Lake Malawi diocese, and found his vocation appreciated up north; here the Malawian bishop gave him the support and training that he needed prior to his ordination in 2016 – fifteen years after our initial conversation!

Carolyn Pickson's story is very different, but peppered with just as much sadness. Her Chinese father seems to have disappeared from the scene at an early stage, abandoning her Malawian mother who subsequently died of AIDS. In her teens she was given a home by a Presbyterian couple from South Korea who worked at Zomba Theological College. When they left for a new mission assignment in Russia in 2000, we moved into the house they had occupied, and of course continued to support Carolyn. She stayed with us until late in 2003, when we returned to Britain. Initially she was completing her schooling in Zomba, and (like Andy) gained her Malawi school certificate. She also looked after her own section of our vegetable garden, where she successfully grew bumper crops of maize. At first her aim was to train as a nurse, but it was the toll of AIDS on her extended family that made her hesitate. Almost every month there would be news of the death of another close relative, and in the end it was the prospect of having so many patients dying of AIDS in a hospital ward that deterred her from a career in nursing. It also discouraged her from any serious relationship that might lead to being married herself, since it was obvious that in Malawi by no means all men were likely to prove faithful to their wives. After leaving school she therefore started to attend typing classes and to equip herself with secretarial skills. She realised too that a secretarial income would enable her to support several of her younger orphaned cousins and to be the much needed bread-winner for her family.

Her new vocation began to take off when she started to work for a missionary colleague who was preparing an English-Chichewa dictionary. This then led to permanent employment within the college precincts as secretary to TEEM (Theological Education by Extension), and later – further down the same road in Zomba – to secretarial roles within Chancellor College (the University of

Malawi). Before we left, we made sure she had what was needed to construct her own house back in her home village a few miles away. Her grandmother, who was the village chief, was then still alive. Carolyn has more recently completed her own degree at the university, and will no doubt become quite a senior administrative figure there.

   Both these personal sketches are not untypical of the process by which many people come to find, not merely a 'job', but a 'calling'. Occasionally this may come 'out of the blue', as with St Paul on the Damascus road, but it should not be supposed that discovering one's true vocation is necessarily quite so dramatic nor even an irresistible inner conviction. God's call may rather be heard (as Newman suggested) through the course of events, through observing the needs of particular individuals or society as a whole ('Whom shall I send and who will go for us?'), or through the wisdom and encouragement of others. Sometimes too, as perhaps for St Matthew at the seat of custom, the way forward emerges after other options have proved consistently unsatisfactory or unfulfilling, although as John Wesley sagely observed (in the Methodist covenant service):

> Christ has many services to be done ... Some are suitable to our inclinations and interests, others are contrary to both. In some we may please Christ and please ourselves, but in others we cannot please Christ except by denying ourselves.

It is a little sad that these days the majority of Catholics will gladly pray for more vocations to the priesthood or to the consecrated life, but would not willingly even hint to their own offspring that these options might be worth exploring (whereas in the past, with much larger families, it was thought a great honour and blessing to have at least one son as a priest or a daughter as a nun).

George and Alfred at Ngope Tsoeu

Freddie with (assistant) Bp Donald on his ordination to the diaconate

SOME of the CPSA's ordinands studying at the new Lelapa La Jesu Seminary at Roma University were photographed by Michael Phalatse when they attended Lesotho's Day of Prayer in Thaba Bosiu on March 16 . . . they are (back row, from left) John Ntsoko (Johannesburg), Freedy Masole (Johannesburg), Aubrey Ntho (Lesotho), (front row, from left) Andrew Matsane (Johannesburg), Mandla Dlamini (Swaziland), Mobau Nkheloane (Lesotho) and Serumo Lebotlane (Lesotho).

Some of the seminarians at Lelapa la Jesu, Roma

On a weekend retreat at Limbe

Visiting Mua Catholic Cultural Centre

A Good Friday Procession of Witness

Gathering in the Wives' School at ZTC

Seminarians (and wives) at Zomba Theological College

St George's, Zomba

A festive day in neighbouring Milepa

Former student Brighton (now bishop)
while i/c Magomero, within Zomba parish

Outside Me` Alice's rondavel
a mountain outstation served from Roma

Mission stations near and far

Both Andy and Carolyn came from religious backgrounds in which accountability for the way one lives or has lived was ever a prominent feature. That was also true in my own Methodist upbringing, where additionally a sharing in the Church's mission was also much esteemed. As a child I was encouraged to join the JMA (Junior Missionary Association), which chiefly meant collecting weekly subscriptions from friends and neighbours to support work abroad. I was also introduced to a series of booklets that offered potted biographies of famous missionaries and some of their converts, and can recall finding them quite inspirational. My academic career, however, seemed to be heading in a different direction, with considerable success in mathematics and indeed a research paper published when I was barely aged 20. There was pressure from the college to continue in this direction, but my own instinct was to get much more involved with people: trying to think clearly and logically is a challenge I enjoy, but it tends to engage the head rather too exclusively. A tragic event also occurred in my second year which may have changed my orientation more than I realised at the time. I was then sharing rooms with a fellow mathematician Peter Lapwood, who one Sunday evening in February 1963 was returning on his bicycle from a preaching assignment at a rural Congregational church; it was an icy road, and he skidded and was killed outright by a following car. I was in shock for several weeks, never having encountered death so starkly before. The college chaplain Keith Sutton, who later on became bishop of Lichfield, was extremely supportive and provided me with a role model that captured my imagination far more than those highly distinguished academics I had met, such as Fred Hoyle who in those days was in the public eye as often as (say) Stephen Hawking came to be in succeeding decades.

I left Cambridge uncertain of my future direction. Initially I opted for school teaching, chiefly to give myself space to ponder but also to engage with congenial colleagues (at Oundle School). As an accredited Methodist local preacher I regularly took Sunday services in the nearby village churches – but on weekdays at the school I became increasingly aware of what seemed, despite compulsory chapel for the boys, to be a spiritual vacuum in many of their lives. During my own time as a teenager, whether at church or in school, emphasis had been placed upon service to others, yet the priorities for the generation I was now teaching seemed to be (in no particular order) money, drink and girls. Something vital seemed to me to be missing – which prompted me to echo Isaiah's response in similar circumstances long ago, 'Here am I Lord, send me'.

The move from school teaching into full-time (Anglican) ministry was not entirely straightforward. I was berated by a fellow Methodist at the school; my parents thought I was wasting my gifts; even the assessors at the selection conference I attended seemed to think that school teachers could do more good in the world than Christian priests (maybe they had a point!); but perseverance paid off in the end. Three years studying theology at Oxford were followed by ordination and over twelve years serving in parishes within the diocese of Peterborough. In both Northampton and Irchester there were significant links with the church overseas which I was glad to encourage (whereas in recent decades a global perspective seems to have diminished within many English parishes?). It is always good to stretch people's outlook, and a priest can do this both by drawing upon Christian resources from previous generations and through present day links that engage with experiences elsewhere.

The opportunity to minister for a time in an African setting had therefore a great appeal for me – a missionary vocation, partnering the local church.

We lift them to the Lord

Bless the Lord, O my soul!
O Lord my God, thou art very great!
Thou art clothed with honour and majesty,
who coverest thyself with light as with a garment,
who hast stretched out the heavens like a tent,
who hast laid the beams of thy chambers on the waters,
who makest the clouds thy chariot,
who ridest on the wings of the wind,
who makest the winds thy messengers,
fire and flame thy ministers.
Thou didst set the earth on its foundations,
so that it should never be shaken.
Thou didst cover it with the deep as with a garment;
the waters stood above the mountains.
Thou makest springs gush forth in the valleys;
they flow between the hills,
By them the birds of the air have their habitation;
they sing among the branches.
(*Psalm 104.1-6,10,12*)

Is it by your wisdom that the hawk soars,
and spreads his wings toward the south?
Is it at your command that the eagle mounts up
and makes his nest on high?
On the rock he dwells and makes his home
in the fastness of the rocky crag.
(*Job 39.26-28*)

 **Martial eagle**   **Wooden fish eagle**

From Malawi

Re li phahamisetsa ho Morena

The Lord reigns; let the earth rejoice;
let the many coastlands be glad!
Clouds and thick darkness are round about him;
righteousness and justice are the foundation of his throne.
(*Psalm 97.1-2*)

The poinsettia (an import from its native Mexico) grows tall in Malawi, reaching higher than potted European versions.
　This can be equally true of the Christian faith in Africa.

The mountains melt like wax before the Lord,
before the Lord of all the earth.
The heavens proclaim his righteousness;
and all the peoples behold his glory.
All worshipers of images are put to shame,
who make their boast in worthless idols;
all gods bow down before him.
Zion hears and is glad,
and the daughters of Judah rejoice,
because of thy judgments, O God.
For thou, O Lord, art most high over all the earth;
thou art exalted far above all gods.
(*Psalm 97.5-9*)

Tiikweza kwa Ambuye

For lo, he who forms the mountains, and
creates the wind,
and declares to man what is his thought;
who makes the morning darkness,
and treads on the heights of the earth --
the Lord, the God of hosts, is his name!
(*Amos 4.13*)

Lord, thou hast been our dwelling place
in all generations.
Before the mountains were brought forth,
or ever thou hadst formed the earth and the world,
from everlasting to everlasting thou art God.
(*Psalm 90.1-2*)

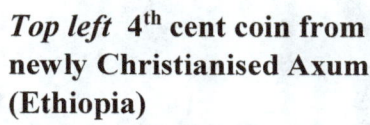

Top left 4th cent coin from newly Christianised Axum (Ethiopia)

Bottom left A craggy hilltop in the high veldt (a gift from Lesotho)

Bottom right How profound is Christian faith in Malawi?

Inculturation

Although within a relatively short time Christianity spread across North Africa, whence emerged outstanding teachers of the faith such as Clement of Alexandria, Tertullian, Cyprian and Augustine, not to mention the rise of Christian monasticism in Egypt, not nearly so much remained (other than in Nubia and Ethiopia) after the collapse of Roman rule and the later Muslim incursion. Nor did the early churches here reflect much of the so-called primal culture associated with the African continent.

A new phase began in the late 15th century when the Portuguese established trading links further south around the African coast. Within a hundred years or so there was missionary activity some way inland – up the Zambezi river, and in what is now Angola – but engagement with indigenous traditions was sporadic, and few Catholic priests troubled to learn much of the local language. This changed quite dramatically in the 19th century when mission work in the African interior began to be promoted on a large scale. There was indeed competition between Protestant societies and newly founded Catholic religious orders. Since the latter had fewer commercial links and less political motivation, they tended to be more sympathetic to existing practices. Thus, the Missionaries of Africa, founded in the 1850s by Cardinal Lavigerie of Algiers, were given explicit instructions by him on the question of 'civilisation':

> Missionaries must not only learn the local language in order to communicate with the people, they must speak it among themselves. The children they educate must be allowed to remain truly African and to keep their customs and their way of life.

Soon afterwards, Daniel Comboni launched the Verona Fathers and Sisters, having first enunciated his Plan for the Regeneration of Africa in 1865. His crucial idea was to regenerate Africa 'by means of Africa herself':

> Settlements will have to be established where young Africans can be trained in their own environment, but preserving their racial characteristics.

Trainees of the Holy Ghost Fathers were likewise reminded that the Christian religion had 'invariably to be established in the soil'.

Yet there were bleaker views within the Vatican itself. In 1873 the Congregation of Indulgences, supported by Pope Pius IX, published a prayer, asking God to take away 'the curse of Ham' from the hearts of 'the most miserable Ethiopian peoples in Central Africa, who form a tenth of humanity'. The prayer clearly implied that 'Christian' Europe was far in advance of the primitive barbarism of Africa – in line with the prevailing 'religious Darwin*ism*' which by now had distorted Darwin's original aim of providing a scientific challenge to racism and slavery.

The response to the new wave of 19th century Christian missionaries by the local African population was mixed. Because of their white skin, Europeans were often identified with the ancestors (but not e.g. among the Herero people of Namibia), and so might be hospitably received as messengers from the world beyond. Yet there was also a wariness about ceding too much influence to outsiders, unless there were perceived benefits. Usually what African rulers looked for was the enhancement of their own 'power', alongside the need for protection against any forces that threatened, whether residing in nature itself, in malevolent spirits or in hostile neighbouring tribes. Thus, in Buganda (in the 1870s) Kabaka Mutesa I agreed to receive Bible lessons from the Calvinist missionaries if they would also arrange a supply of gun powder. His bargaining suggests that missionaries should always be a little cautious in assessing apparent successes or gains. It is certainly disturbing to find some Christian evangelists deliberately promoting a 'prosperity gospel' (the promise of earthly blessings, greater wealth and heavenly rewards for their followers), which is little else than bribery – probably with an eye to their own personal enrichment. Jesus himself counselled his disciples:

> If any man would come after me, let him deny himself and take up his cross and follow me.

It has always moved me to visit the graveyard in Nkhotakota where a number of Anglican missionaries to Malawi are buried. Regardless of the unknown hazards that might arise, they volunteered at a young age for service abroad. It was not for their own glory that they did so, but because they believed their

Christian faith was meant to be shared as widely as possible. They knew full well of the failure of Bishop Mackenzie's original expedition, carried out under David Livingstone's guidance in the 1860s, and of how their settlement at Magomero (later to be part of Zomba parish) had to be abandoned largely because of the deaths brought on by malaria, a poor diet and even worse communications. They had no exaggerated expectations of any rapid church growth in this follow-up mission, which had begun in Zanzibar in 1876 before spreading westwards to the mainland. A number of the gravestones still visible record death occurring before the age of 30, after perhaps just two or three years of active service – yet others replaced them, which is hard to imagine happening in today's world.

One who survived longer, William Percival Johnson, lived very much in the spirit recommended by Fathers Lavigerie and Comboni. His life was sketched briefly in the UMCA publication *A Hero Man* (D.Y. Mills 1931), which describes an almost unbelievable record of setbacks and hardships overcome by sheer persistence, courage and faith. Towards the end of his life Johnson was awarded the degree of Doctor of Divinity by Oxford University, and the citation on that occasion provides us with an overview of his missionary activities:

> The ceremony took place on March 2nd 1910 at the Sheldonian Theatre, Oxford, and among the hundreds of people gathered to do him honour were the bishop of Zanzibar, Dr. Weston, and several members of the Mission.
>
> The Warden of Keble College, in a magnificent speech in Latin, said, among other things, that the Archdeacon was a man who deserved, if anyone ever deserved, to be honoured alike by the Church and by the University, a man gifted with the ability and the courage of a hero. And he went on to tell how, as an undergraduate, he achieved distinction in the schools and very great distinction on the river; how he was planning to enter the

Civil Service in India, when all of a sudden he abandoned his plan, and with it the hope of a glorious career of office, because he had heard the voice of someone appealing to him from afar, 'Come over into Africa and help us'; how he heard, he went over and for five and thirty years he had given his help.

This he had done in more than one way. First and foremost he had made it his object to preach the Gospel to those rough and uncivilised tribes (*sic*) and to gather into one the children of God that were scattered abroad. But while he preached the Gospel, how much else had he achieved!

He told how he had ended feuds, reconciled enemies at war, improved the condition of women, founded schools, educated boys, planted trees, laid out gardens, seen to the building of a steamboat and steered the boat when built. He told of his difficulties and dangers – how he had traversed districts hitherto untrodden by man, swampy morasses, virgin forests, with beasts of prey howling around and enemies on every side threatening his life. How sickness had come upon him and how though he was 'pure in life, unscathed by guilt,' he had not brought his body back unscathed, for one eye was sightless. How whatever he had undertaken he had made up his mind to perform: wherever he had had to go, he had insisted on going, vigorous, active, undismayed, 'inspired with a courage surely given him by heaven'.

And then he went on to tell how he had been honoured by the Royal Geographical Society for his splendid explorations and maps, and how he had found out the Chinyanja language and put it together into a grammar and vocabulary so that other people would be able to learn and understand it and had translated the whole of the Bible into this language to help the Africans. He described how the Archdeacon was determined to go back again and felt that he had done really nothing because there was still so much to do.

Then he said how very glad all the wise men of the University were to give him the greatest honour they could to show how proud they were of all the splendid things he had done. And he concluded his speech with saying: 'I beg leave to introduce the Venerable William Percival Johnson of University College, that he may be admitted to the Degree of Doctor of Divinity, *honoris causa*.' And then there was a tremendous burst of cheering which almost lifted the roof.

Mills gives a particularly detailed account of one of Johnson's most creative innovations – the use of a small steamer on Lake Nyasa (*now Lake Malawi*) as his missionary base for work in the coastal settlements. Back in England in 1884, Johnson had sought support for this project:

> Funds were quickly forthcoming and in October 1884, a small steamer, to be called the *Charles Janson*, was sent out in 380 packages, via the Cape and thence up the Zambesi on a hired tug, and at last put together on the shores of the Lake itself.

Its launch was somewhat delayed, and for a time Johnson suffered ophthalmia whose long term effect was blindness in one eye; but eventually, on September 6th 1885 the ship was dedicated for its future role in the mission. Its first captain (Mr Sherriff) described the usual weekly pattern:

> The steamer is a great help to our Mission work, for our headquarters are on an island about 130 miles up the Lake, called Likoma. There are a great many people living in it and it is only eight miles from the mainland. There is a little bay on Likoma Island where we anchor the steamer on Sundays. We begin the day with a service in the chapel. Then we cross the Lake to the mainland and Mr Johnson goes ashore and speaks to the people at two villages. We then steam down the Lake to the next village and there we stop for the night.
>
> Service at six, start again to the next and so to all the villages down the east side of the Lake: then we get back to Likoma on Friday and land what food we have been able to buy on our journey while Mr Johnson is at the villages. This food is for the boys at our school, of whom we have thirty, and for ourselves. It consists principally of rice flour, corn, sweet potatoes, pumpkins, beans and fowls: sometimes a goat. The men of the crew are paid in cloth and buy their own provisions. Saturdays, start to two other villages in another route, back again at night: Sundays, lay at anchor and go ashore to food and service. We have morning and evening service every day on board, and Holy Communion thrice a week.
>
> I thought to find the Lake very smooth, but I find we get many severe storms, sometimes we cannot steam against them and the thunder and lightning is very severe, and the rain comes down in torrents at this time of the year (December); when the sun is out it is very

hot. Mr Johnson had 150 adults to his meeting at Monkey Bay this morning and many children. We are down here one Sunday out of every four: this is near to where we get our letters left by the African Lakes Corporation.

There are a lot of leopards and deer and monkeys and snakes, but not so many lions and elephants as there are further up the Lake. The people often tell us how the elephants eat all their crops at some of the villages where we call … We have very few mosquitoes, but many other flies and some that bite very hard … snakes too we find at times in the cabin, and I have found scorpions in my bed at night.

Johnson never considered his own comfort. He gave away his clothes, he ate whatever was offered; if he felt ill, he fought against it with all his might. Often when he visited the villages he was ill-treated. People sometimes beat him with sticks and threw dust at him – but, never daunted, he would return again and again even if the reception remained hostile. Every morning he was up before the sun and would go ashore with the least amount of luggage – a bed (in case he had to sleep ashore), pots and pans, books, etc. – carried on the head of a willing convert. His road led him through narrow tracks with bushes and tall grass as high as his head. Arriving at a village he would then hold classes for catechumens or hearers; he might need to settle disputes; he would seek help from villagers in his ongoing work of biblical translation. If possible, he would have a simple church constructed of poles on which mud and dung were plastered, surmounted by a thatched roof. At the close of the day a boy would sound a horn or ring a bell to announce a time of prayer.

After a few years it became clear that the *Charles Janson* was too small to serve the mission's growing needs. The *Chauncy Maples* was launched in 1901; Johnson could now have more Africans on board to train as future teachers or as priests (one of whom was Leonard Kamungu, who served as a missionary in neighbouring Northern Rhodesia). The Archdeacon (as Johnson had now become) also wanted to include women so that female education could be developed; but this never happened, as the steamer was known to be extremely uncomfortable in rough seas – the bishop himself dreaded a voyage when he had to go on any confirmation tour. Johnson continued, of course, to be much concerned with his mission work in roughly 60 lakeside villages.

Much of this eastern shore lies today within Mozambique (although further north is now Tanzania); during the 1980s civil war reached this region and drove many people living here across the lake to take refuge in Malawi. Not all returned, but St Martin's Church, Mala (south-east of Likoma Island) has been rebuilt, and we were fortunate to visit there by boat one Sunday in 2003 while staying not far away. I presided at their mass – in Chichewa, which is now their main language – and learnt that the pioneer on these shores is still remembered as *Saint* Johnson.

In his old age he did not return to England. He was by then 'a tiny figure, wrinkled all over, withered almost to nothing, with a few scattered white hairs, blind in one eye, yet reading every book he could lay his hands on, alert in mind and forceful, yet humble'. It took him three months to go around his scattered district, where there were 5,000 people to teach. The four or more tribes spoke different languages, and two dialects were new to him. Some people lived across the Livingstonia Mountains, more than 9,000 feet high, so his walking must often have been demanding. He lived alone in a simple hut without home comforts, but was especially pleased with his 'roll-top desk' consisting of 'a canvas sack with pockets, stuffed with papers and hung on the mud wall'. He died in 1928, aged 74, at Liuli in Tanzania – UMCA having in 1925 published reminiscences of his early missionary life (as far as 1895).

Archdeacon Johnson buying local food outside his hut in Manda

Our visit to St Martin's Church, Mala (Mozambique) in 2003

With Rodney Hunter in 2001

Building a rondavel in 1985

Dancing from Chimbeta Church 2000

Homemade willow boat, Roma 1985

Walking, dancing, & constructing the local way (in Lesotho & Malawi)

William Johnson is not the only saintly missionary to have served in Central Africa. During our four years in Malawi we came to know Canon Rodney Hunter very well. He had already served for many years as a missionary with UMCA, both in parishes and as a seminary teacher – apart from being my immediate predecessor in Zomba he had also taught at the Catholic seminary of Kachebere. (In Johnson's time, a diary kept by the White Fathers in Malawi noted that 'The Anglicans help us as much as they can and there is no hostility towards us'.) When I first met Rodney in 1999 he was living in Matamangwe in a small house. He lived very simply; he had no car, but either walked around his extensive parish or caught a minibus if he had to travel further afield; he had few household gadgets – his only concession to modernity was a radio-cassette player powered by a car battery. He moved from there to assist in Nkhotakota parish when his health deteriorated a little, so as to be nearer the mission hospital. For a time he returned to England for cancer treatment, but almost as soon as it was completed he was back in his beloved Africa. He came to stay with us in Zomba once or twice each year. Tragically, as noted already, he met his death at the hands of fellow Anglicans in 2006 when he was aged 73. *The Times* had this to say in its obituary a fortnight later:

> The death of Canon Rodney Hunter has deprived the Anglican Church in Central Africa of one of its most senior and distinguished priests … As the decades passed, he seemed ever more clearly to personify the high standard of theological integrity, personal holiness and pastoral devotion for which the Universities' Mission has been rightly acclaimed.

Although (like William Johnson) Rodney Hunter exemplified the vital 'incarnational' principle of rooting his own lifestyle 'in the local soil', he was not, however, much taken with ideas of *liturgical* inculturation. It was Pope

John XXIII, by training a church historian, who in *Princeps Pastorum* (1959) sketched out the radical concept of a multicultural church:

> She does not identify herself with any one culture to the exclusion of the rest – not even with European and Western culture, with which her history is so closely linked ... (She) is ever ready to recognise and acknowledge – and indeed to sponsor whole-heartedly – everything that can be set to the credit of the human mind and spirit ... Wherever real values of art and thought are capable of enriching the human family, the Church is ready to encourage such work of the spirit.

This new perspective was honed further in the epoch-making documents of the 2nd Vatican Council (1962-65):

> We turn our thoughts to all those who acknowledge God and preserve in their traditions precious elements of religion and humanity. We wish that a frank dialogue may lead us all to welcome the impulses of the Spirit and to carry them out courageously ... [Christians should] acknowledge, preserve and encourage the spiritual and moral truths found among non-Christians, also their social life and culture ... Liturgical reforms must ... be open to the genuine pastoral needs of the individual churches.

Most famously, it was Paul VI speaking after the Council to African bishops gathered in Kampala in 1969 who asserted, 'You may, and you must, have an African Christianity'. Or as his successor John Paul II said in Lagos in 1982, 'The Church comes to bring Christ; she does not come to bring the culture of another race'. In Nairobi he was even more specific: 'Christ, in the members of his Body, is himself an African.' This implies that African culture should be 'transformed and regenerated by the gospel' so that it 'brings forth from its own living tradition original expressions of Christian life, celebration and thought'.

Since then African theologians have sought to identify aspects of their own culture which deserve greater emphasis. James Okoye, who grew up in Nigeria, agrees with the Catholic bishops of that region that Africa's cultural affinities are far more with the Jewish roots of Christianity than with its subsequent Hellenistic developments. In particular, he singles out its *oral* culture 'which uses words for communicating feeling and beauty'. 'The Roman liturgy', he suggests, 'privileges doctrine; Africa privileges experience'. Repetition, rather than over-succinct phraseology, would in his view be a more African form of verbal expression. Others (this time in East Africa) have noted the important role of *proverbs* in the initiation of young people within traditional African societies, and have suggested that this style of teaching takes us back to Jesus' own use of parables – a more imaginative and thought-provoking form of instruction than some of the didactic methods commonly used in Christian catechesis or in preaching. And some African proverbs certainly challenge the listener more profoundly than many a verse of the Bible's wisdom literature.

The following text (which provoked a lively response) was an attempt of mine in Zomba to 'inculturate' the Sunday sermon. Its aim was to encourage the seminarians to do better!

> When God made the world he planted mango trees everywhere. All year round, wherever you went – even if far from home – there were ripe mangoes waiting to be picked. But as time went on, there were more and more humans, and not enough mangoes: so some people went mango raiding. They would strip trees in other villages, and leave nothing for the local people or for those passing by. Bad feelings and much fighting ensued, and God said, 'Enough of this! There shall be a law of mangoes. I now decree that you may only pick mangoes that grow within a thousand paces of your home.' This law was a good thing, because it tried to restore peace and bring order. But it also tempted people to go out at night and steal fruit without being seen – so there was less fighting but more suspicion, and hardship for those who kept the law. So what was God to do? He thought of making an extra law, forbidding people to travel more than a thousand paces from their homes. But he

realised that with more restrictions there would only be more lawlessness. Maybe instead he should blight all the mango trees, which would certainly prevent any fruit being stolen? Yet again he thought, people would starve, and find no joy in life, so he stayed his hand.

Instead, he hatched a less obvious plan. His son, whose name was Joshua in Hebrew, went to live quietly in a village for thirty years, never going very far and never stealing anything himself, although he certainly knew mango raiders came and went all the time, causing anger and mayhem. Then an idea came to him. He suggested to his friends that, in their several villages, they should each keep a stock of mangoes ready in baskets for any outsiders to help themselves. They thought this was quite crazy, but they tried it. At first it seemed to work: the raids died down. But then, greed got the upper hand: 'We've only to kill whoever it is puts these mangoes out, and the rest will be ours for good'. Word of this plot spread quickly, and Joshua's friends went into hiding. Not so Joshua himself: 'Take my mangoes, take me too,' he said. Thus his fate was sealed, and things seemed just as bad as ever. Yet to their astonishment, Joshua reappeared dramatically in the very place where his friends were hiding. 'When we gave the mangoes away, did you go hungry? When you lost me, did you think that was the end? You must have faith – and courage to go on giving and sharing.' They then emerged from hiding, and went out to share whatever they had – mangoes and all, whatever the cost – in order to bring peace to God's world.

Words, of course, are not everything – and in a Church that emphasises the sacraments as a means of 'holy communication' it is appropriate that the *whole* person is engaged in both worshipping and witnessing. In Africa the joy of the Gospel is naturally expressed in bodily acts such as *singing* and *dancing*, as also in forms of *artistic* creation. 'Dancing' in a Malawian context may mean little more than swaying the body – and perhaps clapping – while joining in a song, although communal processions are much enlivened when stepped out in rhythm. African singing can also be an uplifting experience, especially when the different voices break so readily into harmony. (It helps not to have an organ accompaniment, which often dictates an unattainably high pitch for the voices!)

Fr Claude Boucher

Born in Quebec in 1941, 'Chisale' (his Nyau name) came to Mua as a White Father in 1967. He founded this centre in 1976 as a cooperative for wood carvers. It grew to encompass the Chamare Museum (featuring Chewa, Ngoni and Yao cultures) and other institutions. He has always sought to create mutual understanding where before there was hostility and suspicion.

Kungoni Centre of Culture and Art (Mua Mission, Malawi)

An African version of the Feeding of the Five Thousand

The compatibility, and possible integration, of Christianity with more deep-seated cultural or religious practices in Africa is less straightforward. Much credit in Malawi must go to the lifelong work of Fr Claude Boucher at the Mua Catholic Mission. We were fortunate when visiting in 2001 to be given a tour of Chamare Museum (actually three separate rondavels) by Fr Boucher himself. By this time the museum was well established, as was his own acceptance by adherents to the local Nyau cult. The advent of Christian missionaries in the late 19th or early 20th centuries had initially been met with suspicion, and more than once it was only a chance occurrence which eased the tension. Thus, on their arrival at Nsanje in 1901, the leading Montfort Father selected the most imposing baobab tree in the village and placed a medallion of Mary on its trunk, entrusting Malawi to her: for the Chewa people who witnessed this act, however, it must have seemed as if these newcomers were making on offering to the local spirits, since for generations they had been placing their own gifts at the foot of this very tree. Likewise, when the White Fathers arrived further south in the middle of a prolonged drought, they held a novena of prayer for the blessing of rain. On the third day, the rain indeed began to fall, convincing the local people of the power and efficacy of this new religion.

What though did the missionaries make of the indigenous rituals? At first, especially when strange masks were worn, they must have seemed quite alien to the Christian faith. Yet, as Fr Boucher came to discover, there were elements with considerable spiritual resonance – such as this Ngoni creation myth:

> Once upon a time there was a God *Umkulukulu*, the Lord of the Sky. Beneath the flat disk of earth stood four bulls carrying the world on their horns and causing earthquakes when they moved. Up in the sky, God was surrounded with a vast entourage of sons and daughters. One young mischievous son had taken the habit of riding God's favourite ox.

Umkulukulu was displeased and decided to send him to earth as a punishment. He had him lowered down, tied with cattle intestines around the waist. On his descent the boy was so stunned by the earth's beauty that he stretched out his hand for a piece of reed and used a splinter to cut himself free from the sky. God soon felt pity for him, and granted him a wife chosen from among the most beautiful girls of the sky. They became the first couple on earth, and gave birth to the *Ngoni* people; but truly they were from above, the *Amazulu*.

When the Maseko *Ngoni* dance in full regalia, they recall their origin from the sky. The men wear the *Njobo*, a beaded navel belt from which a beaded 'umbilical' cord hangs. This symbolizes their descent from above. Their headgear too is made of colourful feathers, like those of birds flying high. And so, when death comes to the *Ngoni*, although their bodies are buried in the earth below, they believe their spirits will ascend to heaven as *Amadlosi*.

This myth differs from the biblical account, but it shares a conviction that we are truly children of God, destined to be with him one day in a realm above. To this belief in the afterlife, there are other features of 'primal' cultures across Africa that are potentially compatible with Christian teaching:

- belief in a supreme (creator) God;
- traditional prayers and titles of God (along with appropriate symbolism);
- sacred shrines;
- belief in the existence of spirits;
- religious cults catering for the emotional needs of people;
- bonds between the living and their deceased relatives;
- prayer to ancestors in times of crisis;
- a strong sense of community, that is, of mutual belonging;
- the importance of family and extended family;
- initiation rites at different stages of life;
- rites of purification for individuals and communities;
- times of festival and celebration such as harvest.

Thus, Africans traditionally see an inseparable bond between life and religion.

Several of these features that are so important on the African continent are clearly uncontroversial for the Church – and indeed are universally accepted (family and community life and the celebration of festivals, for example). Others have their Christian counterparts, and there is much to be gained by exchanging ideas and maybe also by adopting certain elements of what is practised. The emphasis upon the 'personal' is of particular value in Western society where isolation is growing rapidly, while face-to-face communication is diminishing. In Malawi, if one entered any gathering – large or small – as a stranger, most if not all of those present would offer their own welcome and introduce themselves; in England, one might too often shrink unnoticed into a quiet corner of the room! Indeed, most African countries have some equivalent to the Zulu saying, *Umuntu ngumuntu nagabantu*, or as a Tumbukan proverb from Northern Malawi puts it, 'A person is a person because of neighbours'. Yet this begs the question posed in the Gospels, to which Jesus responded in his parable of the Good Samaritan: 'Who is my neighbour?' The problem highlighted earlier is that in Africa (as in many other places, including Britain) the boundaries of neighbourliness can be too narrowly drawn, and outside one's own tribe, however that is defined, others are not truly recognised as 'persons'.

Although some features of Malawian culture are fading under outside influence (or being maintained solely to entertain tourists), it is understandable that their very strangeness was a challenge to the first missionaries. This is certainly true of adolescent initiation practices (such as the role of the so-called *fisi* – the 'hyena' - who introduced girls to sexual intercourse). *Gule Wamkulu* (see overleaf) also seemed dangerous because of its dramatic personification of evil – but it was perhaps no less intimidating than Dante's *Inferno* or the many church murals depicting the Last Judgement.

Gule Wamkulu *is a secret Chewa cult, involving a ritual dance performed by the 'Nyau' brotherhood. The dance concludes the initiation of young men into adult society, usually soon after the harvest has been gathered. Gule Wamkulu can also be seen at weddings, funerals, and the installation or death of a chief. The Nyau dancers wear costumes and masks made of wood and straw, representing characters such as wild animals, spirits of the dead, slave traders (but also more recent figures - such as a helicopter!). Their role is to teach the audience moral and social values. The figures perform their dances with extraordinary energy, entertaining and scaring the audience as representatives of the world of the spirits and the dead, some good and many evil.*

Gule Wamkulu

(Listed in 2008 by UNESCO as an "Intangible Cultural Heritage of Humanity")

Outside Africa it is not always appreciated how much importance attaches to the ancestors, even when pressing political matters may be assumed to dominate attention. I was surprised myself at an ecumenical conference held in Grahamstown in 1985 at the height of the apartheid years how much more concern was expressed about cultural issues than about justice, freedom and reconciliation. The greatest stress was laid upon the need to express affinity with the ancestors, who 'having passed through death ... share in mystical powers not ordinarily available to those presently alive'. It is customary in Africa for the ancestors, who are seen as mediators in helping people to be fertile, healthy and prosperous and are regarded as the guardians of their earthly relatives, always to be consulted about family matters and personal decisions, if possible by paying a visit to their graves and making a tangible offering of foodstuff or some libation. Their response is revealed subsequently in dreams and premonitions, or perhaps in striking omens; these may require consultation with a diviner. The African is apparently far closer here to the biblical and ancient world than is his European counterpart, and the disparagement of the ancestors by mission churches has certainly been a major factor in the rise of many AICs (African Initiated Churches). One example is the formation in 1955 in Namibia of *Okereka Jevangeli Joruuana*, that is, the Herero Church. The Herero suspected that veneration of ancestors was really being rejected by whites as part of a drive to deprive them of their nationhood.

That does not, however, rule out some rapprochement between African recourse to 'the ancestors' and Christian veneration of the saints – especially since a true ancestor was not just any forebear, but one who lived a worthy life, who was blessed with offspring and provided for them. Yet although the saints were (in most cases!) worthy, their prayers are surely for all who need them.

Christians of whatever tribe or race may seek their intercession, whereas the ancestors look primarily to their own kith and kin. We recall too that Christians have been taught by Jesus, especially in the *Our Father*, to approach God directly; in fact Christ himself, so we are told, 'always lives to make intercession' (Hebrews 7.25); whilst St Paul reminds us that 'God has sent the Spirit of his Son into our hearts, crying 'Abba! Father!' (Galatians 4.6).

Several points may be added here. A broader discussion concerns those who died without confessing the Christian faith or indeed without being baptised: the approach to pagan ancestors has certainly changed under the influence of Karl Rahner's doctrine of the *anonymous Christian*. Again, John Paul II once suggested that veneration of ancestors may be 'in some way a preparation for belief in the communion of the saints', describing African beliefs here as 'traditions open to the Gospel' and 'open to the truth'.

Thus, the interaction between the Christian faith and prevailing religious beliefs continues to develop. The haunting question (asked by our now deceased friend Patrick Kalilombe) is 'whether Christians have recognised African spirituality as a potential ally in the struggle against the worst aspects of colonial and neo-colonial infection?' He notes here the tendency to see success in the modern world as 'dependent mainly upon the individual's own efforts and personal ambition, rather than on community cooperation and sharing'. It is a view, he argues, that 'puts a premium on aggressive and self-interested competition'. What Africans consider as primary is 'the value of good and harmonious human relationships'. Where relationships break down, he sees a tendency in Africans to seek revenge, while in the West people often withdraw from further communication. It is clear that the need for Christian forgiveness is by no means confined to any one continent or ethnicity!

Let us give thanks to the Lord our God

For the Lord your God is bringing you into a good land, a land of brooks of water, of fountains and springs, flowing forth in valleys and hills, a land of wheat and barley, of vines and fig trees and pomegranates, a land of olive trees and honey, a land in which you will eat bread without scarcity, in which you will lack nothing, a land whose stones are iron, and out of whose hills you can dig copper.

And you shall eat and be full, and you shall bless the Lord your God for the good land he has given you.
(*Deuteronomy 8.7-10*)

Left A mountain village in Lesotho
  (tapestry woven in Teyateyaneng)

Below A village scene *(drawn by Patrica aged 5)*

From thy lofty abode thou waterest the mountains;
the earth is satisfied with the fruit of thy work.
Thou dost cause the grass to grow for the cattle,
and plants for man to cultivate,
that he may bring forth food from the earth,
and wine to gladden the heart of man,
oil to make his face shine,
and bread to strengthen man's heart.
The trees of the Lord are watered abundantly,
the cedars of Lebanon which he planted.
In them the birds build their nests;
the stork has her home in the fir trees.
The high mountains are for the wild goats;
the rocks are a refuge for the badgers.

Man goes forth to his work
and to his labour until the evening.
O Lord, how manifold are thy works!
In wisdom hast thou made them all;
the earth is full of thy creatures.
(*Psalm 104.13-18, 23-24*)

Lesotho villages pictured by Sarah and Gabriel

A re leboheng Morena Molimo oa rona

And Elijah arose, and ate and drank, and went in the strength of that food forty days and forty nights to Horeb the mount of God. And there he came to a cave, and lodged there; and behold, the word of the Lord came to him, and he said to him, "Go forth, and stand upon the mount before the Lord." And behold, the Lord passed by, and a great and strong wind rent the mountains, and broke in pieces the rocks before the Lord, but the Lord was not in the wind; and after the wind an earthquake, but the Lord was not in the earthquake; and after the earthquake a fire, but the Lord was not in the fire; and after the fire a still small voice.
(*1 Kings 19.8-9, 11-12*)

Left **Baobab tree in Malawi, a focus for primal religious rites**

Right **Bushman cave painting in Lesotho, with spiritual resonances**

And after six days Jesus took with him Peter and James and John, and led them up a high mountain apart by themselves; and he was transfigured before them, and his garments became glistening, intensely white, as no fuller on earth could bleach them. And there appeared to them Elijah with Moses; and they were talking to Jesus. And Peter said to Jesus, "Master, it is well that we are here; let us make three booths, one for you and one for Moses and one for Elijah." For he did not know what to say, for they were exceedingly afraid. And a cloud overshadowed them, and a voice came out of the cloud, "This is my beloved Son; listen to him." (*Mark 9.2-7*)

Above **Malawi drummer, simultaneously singing and dancing** – *a Trinitarian image (the Father keeps the round world throbbing, the Son proclaims his Word, the Holy Spirit infuses new life and hope)*

Left **Lesotho tapestry hanging behind the altar in St Andrew's chapel, Roma** (*designed by Peter Hancock*)

Timthokoze Ambuye Mulungu wathu

In the beginning was the Word, and the Word was with God, and the Word was God. He was in the beginning with God; all things were made through him, and without him was not anything made that was made. In him was life, and the life was the light of men. The true light that enlightens every man was coming into the world. He was in the world, and the world was made through him, yet the world knew him not. He came to his own home, and his own people received him not. But to all who received him, who believed in his name, he gave power to become children of God; who were born, not of blood nor of the will of the flesh nor of the will of man, but of God. And the Word became flesh and dwelt among us, full of grace and truth.
(*John 1.1-4, 9-14*)

Above **Malawi crib scenes**   **Below left** **Swazi candle**   **Below right** **Wilderness chapel**

John went into all the region about the Jordan, preaching a baptism of repentance for the forgiveness of sins. As it is written in the book of the words of Isaiah the prophet, "The voice of one crying in the wilderness: Prepare the way of the Lord, make his paths straight. Every valley shall be filled, and every mountain and hill shall be brought low, and the crooked shall be made straight, and the rough ways shall be made smooth; and all flesh shall see the salvation of God."
(*Luke 3.3-6*)

Butterflies, flowers, and gentle scenery breathing peace in and beyond Lesotho

Globalisation

The two African countries in which we resided (Lesotho, then much later Malawi), although politically, culturally, and geographically quite different from each other, were nevertheless not entirely dissimilar in their past history. A common point of reference is the turmoil created in the 1820s by the rising military dictatorship of the Zulu chief Shaka. This displaced neighbouring tribes who fled from his *mfecane*; the repercussions were experienced both near and far, with rival groups seeking new territory for themselves further afield. Eventually a relatively minor chief Moshoeshoe gained ascendancy over other migrant tribes, and brought their scattered remnants together as the Basotho nation. He is seen on the bank note above in an 1860 portrait wearing a distinctly European top hat. On the left is king Moshoeshoe II, dressed as a middle-class business man (he was the 'constitutional monarch' in the 1980s), while his son Letsie, who assumed the throne on his death, has reasserted his African identity. By the 1860s Moshoeshoe had surrendered territory previously held further west to European settlers from Cape Colony, and in 1871 what remained of Basutoland became a British protectorate. Independence came in 1966, with Lesotho governed by an elected parliament. Yet it was by no means economically self-sufficient: more than 50% of national income was resourced in neighbouring South Africa, where a high proportion of Basotho men laboured in the mines, leaving women and children to work the fields and tend any animals. The need for cooking and heating fuel, along with the overgrazing of land, then resulted in the steady disappearance of mountainous vegetation – in stormy weather, torrential rain would wash soil from the mountain slopes and create dongas in the lowlands. This led to a movement of population into urban shacks around Maseru, where former rural small-holders hoped (often in vain) to gain employment. Brothels and beer-houses became more numerous, and over 30% of the active population became infected with HIV/AIDS. The Highlands Water Project, long-debated in our time because of security issues, was at last implemented, resulting in several villages being flooded; although the main beneficiary was South Africa's water supply, Lesotho did gain certain improvements to its infrastructure. One other development which we noticed on our visit in 2008 was an influx of Chinese, running local stores and some clothing factories. Nearly half of Lesotho's exports in the form of clothing and diamonds then end up in the United States; and given that the bulk of its imports also come from the U.S. via South Africa, there are economists and politicians over there who consider that increasing foreign aid to Lesotho will certainly benefit America – never mind any good it may or may not bring to Lesotho's struggling population!

Malawi's history is very different, but there are some features it has in common with that of Lesotho. Whereas it was trekkers (both Boers and British) crossing the Orange River in ox-waggons who came to occupy some of the latter's territory, it was at first Portuguese traders seeking ivory and gold, later joined by Omani Arabs looking for slaves, who made inroads into the 'Maravi' kingdom from the 16th century onwards. With the 19th century decline in the Atlantic slave trade, the East African supply built up to previously unreached proportions. It is estimated that an annual total of 10,000 or more slaves passed through each of the main depots, Nkhotakota and (at the southern end of the lake) Mponda, during the peak years of the 1860s. The Yao tribe, who had acquired guns a couple of decades earlier, collaborated with the trade, constantly threatening nearby Chewa and Nyanja people; likewise, the Ngoni, who had come north as a result of Shaka's reign of terror, added to their misery with several savage massacres. It was in the Ntchisi Hills, west of Nkhotakota, that many took refuge at this time.

By coincidence, David Livingstone had now begun to discover routes into the African interior, and reported back home the opportunities he saw in Central Africa – rich in minerals, fertile for cultivation, and with navigable rivers made for trade, there was 'an open path for commerce and Christianity'. The 'Christian' response came first, but met with more problems than Livingstone had foreseen and made a faltering start. Again, although the Lancashire cotton mills were looking for alternative raw materials, given the hitches arising from the American Civil War, they soon discovered that the Zambezi belt did not lend itself (as Livingstone had claimed) to cotton growing. It was in the late 1870s that the Scottish Moir brothers set up their African Lakes Corporation with the aim of opening river traffic to and from the coast, along with trading around Lake Malawi (thus offering a commercial alternative to the slave trade). Before the end of the century settlers encouraged by Cecil Rhodes had also reached the Shire Highlands, where their most successful cash crop was tobacco – which is still the case today. Cash crops became a necessity for Africans too, as in the new Central African Protectorate workers were required to pay 'hut taxes': about a quarter of adult males became seasonal migrant labourers in Rhodesia or South Africa.

During the 2nd World War, as during the 1st, Africans were conscripted (on very low rates of pay) into the British army. The post-war period unsurprisingly saw widespread questioning as to whether colonial occupation served the local population at all adequately, and after political protests and strikes (with some prominent Malawians imprisoned for a time) independence came to Nyasaland in 1964, and 'Malawi' was born. Agriculture at this time accounted for about 55% of Gross National Product; it was supported strongly by the government, which on the other hand neglected social developments such as better schooling. President Banda's supporters were the chief beneficiaries when they were granted land taken from many smallholders. His policies started to fail some ten years into his presidency – the national debt mounted rapidly when oil prices quadrupled in 1973/4, and severe food shortages were experienced later in the same decade. As debt repayments abroad became unmanageable, the World Bank demanded structural adjustment programmes that insisted on more cash crops being grown for the export market. In 1990/1 earthquakes and flooding – with a severe drought in the following year – inflicted further suffering on the poorest people, and inevitably Banda's position came to be challenged, despite his ruthless suppression of any opposition. The crucial factor in toppling his regime was the withdrawal of non-humanitarian aid.

Multi-party democracy took over in 1994, which indeed brought some benefits to the country. Continuing population growth, however, put further pressure on resources, not relieved by the huge toll of HIV/AIDS in recent decades and the largely unchecked corruption of politicians and civil servants. At the beginning of the new millennium, it was estimated that there were over 750,000 orphans in the country under the age of sixteen, representing at least 7% of the population. It is doubtful how well a Western country would have coped with such a situation, but Malawi's strength continues to lie in its local communities. Most of these orphans did not end up in institutional orphanages, but were cared for in ones and twos in their own neighbourhoods or villages – often by grannies or near relatives, but also by 'foster' parents living close by. This was very evident in the villages near Zomba, as we shall see.

What is generally needed, as many observers including church leaders came increasingly to realise, is a balance between external (or 'global') support and the proper use of local resources. Important teaching documents started to emerge from Catholic commentators in the late 19th century, starting with Leo XIII's landmark encyclical *Rerum Novarum* (1891). In it he proposed the idea of 'the common good': economic considerations must always take human need into account, while social policies should never deny individual liberties nor human rights. A later watchword became 'solidarity linked to subsidiarity': the former implies a shared (national or global) responsibility to work for the betterment of all; the latter insists – as in *Quadragesimo Anno* (1931) – that 'it is gravely wrong to take from individuals what they can accomplish by their own initiative and industry'.

Our main aim as missionaries serving in Africa was thus to *support* local people and their communities – in strengthening their faith, in discovering their own vocations, and in exercising their gifts more effectively. It tallied with the call of bishops meeting a few decades earlier in Rome, who urged:

> Action on behalf of justice and participation in the transformation of the world fully appear to us as a constitutive dimension of the preaching of the Gospel.

Justice certainly requires a fairer distribution of the earth's resources. It is scandalous that today a small group of billionaires control as much wealth as half of the world's population. In Malawi itself, the richest 20% are thirty or forty times better off than the poorest 20%. Yet 'poverty' is a word with a spectrum of meanings: at one end of it are those who face starvation and every kind of deprivation, and at the opposite end those whom social scientists would term 'relatively' poor in comparison with those living around them. In between, there may be those with sufficient to survive, but who lack education or opportunity, or perhaps the support of friends or family. There is emotional poverty and spiritual poverty as well as the scarcity of essential bodily requirements. In Britain, for example, few of those living in a high-rise block of flats in some inner city area may be on the bread-line, yet many social ills such as loneliness, fear and crime may abound; whereas in a 'poor' Malawian village there may nonetheless be the joy of human companionship and a ready sharing of scanty resources. The Nobel prize-winning economist Amartya Sen has argued that a universal definition of poverty should include people's capabilities alongside any measure of their income: that is to say, the poor are not simply 'those who do not have' but also 'those who cannot do' – and sometimes those who have much can do little, or vice versa. In his later work Sen helped to create the notion of the Human Development Index to take account of life expectancy and adult literacy as well as income resources and distribution.

Duncan, our recycling agent
He called most days at our house to collect used packaging which he sold in the market

Zomba market, selling local produce
Some stalls offered second-hand clothes or goods made from metallic waste

Amayi Mpesi looking after orphans
Ntiya lies west of Zomba, near an army base (so with heightened HIV risk)

Maize-meal distribution at Songani
Over 400 orphans in villages east of Zomba were cared for in this project

Local initiatives in and around Zomba

It is not without significance that two effective community projects in the villages we knew near Zomba were both initiated by devout Christians – Amayi Mpesi (a Catholic) in Ntiya and Kennedy Mpoya (an Adventist) in Songani..

The former (whose daughter we knew at St George's) made the care of AIDS sufferers, their offspring and their orphans, her personal responsibility and received helpful training through the local authority. She took Sarah to see some of her people in their homes (often little more than shelters). Rose, for example, was a young mother with four children. When her husband discovered she was HIV positive and seriously ill with TB he simply abandoned her. Her mother then largely cared for the children – along with six others as well.

By contrast, Clement and Gloria were teenage sibling orphans with no one left in their family to help them. They lived in a small outhouse next to the decaying huts where they were brought up. These once constituted a homestead for their grandparents, but in Malawi it was still common to follow the tradition of not dwelling in a deceased person's house. Amayi Mpesi agreed to be their guardian, and was able to provide extra maize and some clothing. Gloria's death from AIDS was not long in coming; after only a few months with the illness she became frail and sickly, and found life a constant day-to-day struggle.

Amayi Mpesi also provided nursery care on weekdays. She was enabled to get a thatched shelter built for the nursery and to buy extra food for the children through the generosity of two young English visitors to Zomba. Sarah too provided bundles of second-hand clothes bought in local markets. But there were frustrations as well: when two truckloads of relief maize arrived in Ntiya, only members of President Muluzi's own political party were allowed to have any. Another disappointment was that out of several bore holes dug for the provision of clean water, three soon became unusable.

Kennedy Mpoya at Songani with several orphans

***Kennedy Mpoya** (an Adventist Christian) became aware in the 1990s of the alarming number of deaths in his village. As a counsellor at St Luke's Hospital, Malosa he realised that, with the hospital often needing (for reasons of limited space) to send AIDS patients home, many of them were then unable to cope either with their own needs or with any children in their family. He rallied the villagers and offered to coordinate their responses to the growing crisis. As the name **Songani Community Care Group** implies, it is the extended community that is involved. The scheme came to cover some ten villages to the east of Zomba and to include far more than the initial 20 orphans: when Sarah first knew Mr Mpoya there were already 350, which grew to 450 within two years. Over 200 households provided homes to one or more of these children. Many other helpers, based in four district centres, made a personal donation of 7 kwacha each week, as well as looking after the youngest children in two nursery centres and growing maize on a couple of plots of land to help feed those in greatest need.*

A sewing project for girls
Teaching home craft skills

A carpentry project for boys
Mosquito screens were fitted at a hospital

Tins made here sold well locally
Practical skills also included bricklaying

War on Want funded the cost of five cows
Older boys helped to build the dairy sheds

Songani Community Care Group provided various 'life skills'
And helped to pay secondary school fees for older orphans

On the opposite side of Zomba, Kennedy Mpoya's care programme covered a much wider area and involved many more helpers and orphans. At Songani every effort was made to keep children of primary-age at school (free in Malawi at this level, except for the cost of a school uniform), and to raise money to pay for the older ones to attend secondary school. Once or twice a month all the orphans received a bar of soap, and those not yet at school were given a meal each day of *likuni phala* (a mixture of soya, flour, maize, with some sugar).

Several local village craftsmen were also engaged regularly to teach life skills such as carpentry, welding and brick laying, with the girls learning how to sew and to make (or alter) clothes. Without parents of their own, the traditional learning acquired in daily family life needed to be imparted in other ways. None the less, older children had to assume many extra responsibilities – caring for their siblings and fulfilling basic needs by fetching water, hoeing the 'garden', and performing so-called menial tasks. Even while one of their parents was weakening steadily with AIDS, they had to shoulder a disproportionate share of the burden of care.

Orphans living in or near Songani were fortunate to have such a far-sighted person as Mr Mpoya in their midst. He was meticulous in checking and recording all the details of (e.g.) finance and attendance, and brought professional training to bear upon the project. Elsewhere, such skills and commitment were less readily available, as evidenced by the number of children begging on the streets of Malawi's main towns. Efforts by NGOs to provide for them and to give them schooling were generally less successful, as the rewards of begging had a more immediate appeal (but alas! today's beggars may be tomorrow's criminals and drug pushers). Kennedy Mpoya's aim was to equip his local youngsters with resources for a more secure and hopeful future.

The greatest challenge came early in 2002, and again in 2003, during the 'hunger months' (January through to March) when reserves from the previous year were very low. Until the new harvest each April many people had only one meal a day – perhaps just roots, grasses or snakes. Heavy rains and flooding in 2001 had resulted in poor maize yields, whose price therefore escalated – a 50kg sack might have cost 250 kwacha soon after harvesting, but six months later would be 850 kwacha. The latter implied a monthly feeding budget at Songani of about £600 (£1.50 per child). On top of this, money was needed for Mr Mpoya to hire a lorry when he went in search of food supplies after the depot at Blantyre, initially stocked with imported grain, ran dry. Friends in England responded generously to our appeal for funds, so the feeding programme was enabled to continue. When Mr Mpoya heard that rice was still available in villages near Lake Chirwa he set off in pouring rain determined to find it, and was successful in buying 26 x 70kg sacks of rice – a fortnight's supply which cost roughly £330. As he returned, the lorry kept getting stuck in the muddy track, leaving no alternative but to unload the sacks in order to get the vehicle moving again. This whole operation had to be repeated several times over the return journey of 20 miles, so that the expedition lasted 12 hours in all. The rice was distributed the next day, and proved a popular alternative to maize.

When – for the time being – the food crisis subsided, two ambitious projects to benefit the local villages were begun. Cow sheds were constructed, and soon one of the cows (funded by War on Want in the UK) calved successfully. Work also started on a maize mill, which would in time generate a steady income. Since 2005, when antiretroviral drugs were introduced into the country, the HIV/Aids situation has improved greatly – the death rate is much less, and there are fewer new infections.

It is right and just

And the multitudes asked him, "What then shall we do?"
And he answered them, "He who has two coats, let him share with him who has none; and he who has food, let him do likewise."
Tax collectors also came to be baptized, and said to him, "Teacher, what shall we do?"
And he said to them, "Collect no more than is appointed you."
Soldiers also asked him, "And we, what shall we do?" And he said to them, "Rob no one by violence or by false accusation, and be content with your wages."
(*Luke 3.10-14*)

And all who believed were together and had all things in common;
and they sold their possessions and goods and distributed them to all, as any had need.
And day by day, attending the temple together and breaking bread in their homes, they partook of food with glad and generous hearts.
(*Acts 2.44-46*)

The communal life of a village in rural Malawi *including brick-making, thatching, cooking, and pounding maize.*

Hoa tsoanela ho mo leboha le ho mo rorisa

Every good endowment and every perfect gift is from above, coming down from the Father of lights with whom there is no variation or shadow due to change.
(*James 1.17*)

Treasures from several African countries *including*
**a reed brush from Mozambique
a thatching needle, a grain scoop
and a hat from Lesotho
an ebony pot from Namibia
a wooden jar and a cedar box from Malawi
a winnowing basket from Swaziland**
together with
**silverware, embroidery and leatherwork
from Nigeria
beaded and carved sticks from Transkei
& a pottery dish from Morocco**

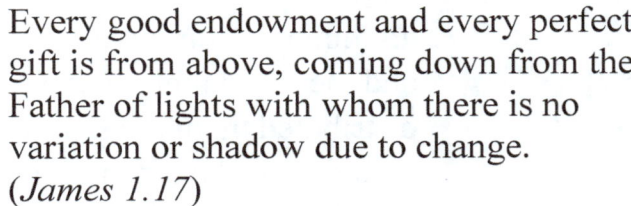

Let the earth bless the Lord;
sing praise to him and highly exalt him for ever.
Bless the Lord, mountains and hills,
sing praise to him and highly exalt him for ever.
Bless the Lord, all things that grow on the earth,
sing praise to him and highly exalt him for ever.
Bless the Lord, you springs,
sing praise to him and highly exalt him for ever.
Bless the Lord, seas and rivers,
sing praise to him and highly exalt him for ever.
Bless the Lord, you whales and all creatures that move in the waters,
sing praise to him and highly exalt him for ever.
(*Song of Azariah 52-57*)

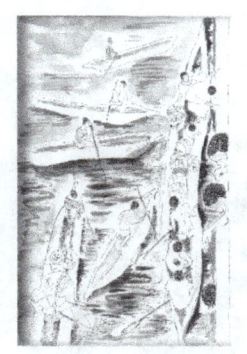

Fishing and trading scenes by Lake Malawi

Kuli koyenera ife ndi kwabwino kuchita chotere

A good wife who can find?
She is far more precious than jewels.
She puts her hands to the distaff,
and her hands hold the spindle.
She opens her hand to the poor,
and reaches out her hands to the needy.
She is not afraid of snow for her household,
for all her household are clothed in scarlet.
She makes herself coverings;
her clothing is fine linen and purple.
(*Proverbs 31.10, 19-22*)

Bless the Lord, you sons of men,
>   *sing praise to him and highly exalt him for ever.*
> Bless the Lord, O Israel,
>   *sing praise to him and highly exalt him for ever.*
> Bless the Lord, you priests of the Lord,
>   *sing praise to him and highly exalt him for ever.*
> Bless the Lord, you servants of the Lord,
>   *sing praise to him and highly exalt him for ever.*
> Bless the Lord, spirits and souls of the righteous,
>   *sing praise to him and highly exalt him for ever.*
> Bless the Lord, you who are holy and humble in heart,
>   *sing praise to him and highly exalt him for ever.*
> (*Song of Azariah 60-65*)

"Small is beautiful"

Both the interior and exterior of traditional rondavels in Lesotho were well cared for, and quite often they were decorated artistically using local materials (especially earth and animal dung, suitably coloured). Domestic utensils and equipment would also be fashioned on site or at least in the same village (before mass-produced items from China and elsewhere flooded the markets). This was true throughout Africa: the treasured items displayed on previous pages were carved, moulded, woven or painted by craftsmen up and down the continent.

In crowded urban settings it is never so easy to achieve the same results; hence dwellings are often makeshift shacks, liable to be demolished when planners or politicians have different ideas. Nevertheless, in any locality it is still possible for communities to thrive – provided they are resourceful enough in other ways, and have sufficient stamina and mutual concern to work together.

Village life in Lesotho (and Malawi, *bottom right*)

Bishop Patrick Kalilombe

African house church in an urban setting

Patrick Kalilombe *(1933–2012) has been described as a 'visionary and progressive' Catholic bishop. He grew up at Mua, and was the first Malawian priest to be a White Father missionary. He became bishop of Lilongwe in 1972 at a time when President Kamuzu Banda was becoming ever more a ruthless dictator. He borrowed ideas of 'liberation theology' from South America, and encouraged 'small parish groups' within his diocese. These brought Christians together within a locality (which might be urban as well as rural) both for their mutual support and to discover the contemporary implications of their faith. Banda, however, regarded these as 'clandestine subversive groups' and in 1976 put Patrick under house arrest. He resigned as bishop in 1979, and it was as an exile in Birmingham that we came to know him prior to our time in Lesotho. He lectured there on his own Chewa people's religious traditions and saw them as foundational for African Christianity to be properly 'inculturated'. His thinking and his courage came to inspire the other Malawian bishops whose challenge to the regime in 1992 soon caused its collapse. Patrick then returned to Malawi under the democratic regime to teach at Chancellor College in Zomba, where we renewed our acquaintance.*

In apostolic times and for several centuries following, the Christian Church invariably met for worship in much smaller gatherings than were often found later on. Its evangelising successes were also usually the result of personal contacts rather than organised campaigns. St Luke in his *Acts of the Apostles* has repeated references to believers using their own homes for teaching and for worship; St Paul too explicitly mentions 'house churches' in his *Letter to the Romans* as well as in *Colossians* and in *Philemon*. There is little evidence of larger assemblies, other than opportunities grasped either within Jewish synagogues or in outdoor arenas to give account of Christian teachings: the exception seems to be in Ephesus where Paul uses 'the hall of Tyrannus' for two whole years for the same purpose. There is also a reference, dating perhaps from around 185 AD, in the apocryphal *Martyrdom of Paul* to his renting a 'barn' (otherwise translated 'granary' or 'warehouse') outside Rome 'where he and the brethren taught the word of truth'. Perhaps the most renowned account from the 2nd century occurs at the trial of Justin Martyr:

> Rusticus the prefect said, 'Where do you assemble?' Justin said, 'Where each one chooses and can: for do you fancy that we all meet in the very same place? Not so; because the God of the Christians is not circumscribed by place; but being invisible, fills heaven and earth, and everywhere is worshipped and glorified by the faithful.' Rusticus the prefect said, 'Tell me where you assemble, or into what place do you collect your followers.' Justin said, 'I live above one Martinus, at the Timiotinian Bath'. (*Act Just Mart* 2)

Those who assembled at most of these early gatherings could not have been too large a number. In the 1st century the Church seems to have been a network of small communities, perhaps foreshadowed in St Mark's account of the Feeding Miracle, where the five thousand 'sat down in groups, by hundreds and by fifties'. Writing in 1908, Adolf von Harnack identified over fifty places where there is evidence of Christians meeting together during the 1st century; while, even in urbanised Rome, Peter Lampe's book *Christians at Rome in the First Two Centuries* (2003) argues that there was no major centre for worship but rather different 'islands of Christianity' within the city. It is particularly interesting to learn of a rather later house church in North Africa: the one surviving pre-Constantinian inventory of a house church assembly lists forty-nine named people who were arrested near Carthage in 304 AD.

	Saturninus *presbyter*		
Saturninus junior *lector* *adolescens*	Felix *lector*	Hilarianus *infans . . . puer*	Maria *sanctimonialis*
	Female congregation		
Telica (= Tazelita?), Restituta, Prima, Eva, Pomponia, Secunda, Ianuaria, Saturnina, Margarita, Honorata, Regiola, Matrona, Caecilia, Berectina, Secunda, Matrona, Ianuaria, Victoria (*flos virginum*)			
	Male congregation		
Dativus *qui et senator*, Felix, Felix, Rogatianus, Quintus, Maximianus, Rogatianus, Rogatus, Januarius, Cassianus, Victorianus, Vincentius, Caecilianus, Rogatianus, Givalius, Rogatus, Martinus, Clautus, Felix, Maior, Victorianus, Pelusius, Faustus, Dacianus, Emeritus *lector*, Ampelius (librarian?)			

It was of course not long after Diocletian's persecution of the Church that Constantine became emperor, and decided to lend strong support to the Christian faith. Not only did public worship become licit, but basilicas and other large churches were constructed in the 4th century which enabled worshippers to gather in much larger numbers than ever before. Whereas one might describe the early Church as 'a network of small gatherings of believers', three centuries later it was becoming an international institution that wielded much influence and attracted considerable wealth.

Yet 'small' does remain 'beautiful', if only because – as sociological research has discovered – most people cannot easily bond with others in a group that exceeds (approximately) one hundred and fifty in number. Below this threshold communities can maintain themselves without too much by way of structure and organisational control; relationships remain personal, and within the group it is possible to know, to respect, and to cooperate with the majority of the remainder. It is not, in other words, a 'crowd' who are largely anonymous to each other, but an 'extended' family – or more accurately 'God's family'.

This is also deeply rooted in African culture. In their study of San culture *San Spirituality* (2004), J.D. Lewis-Williams and D.G. Pearce offer this comment:

> Those who journeyed into the Kalahari Desert [especially in the 1950s and 1960s] did so in search of stress-free communities from whom Westerners could learn much … Coming from a materialistic Western background [Laurens van der Post] and others were struck by an absence of evidence for inequality in material wealth and overt political power. They found no chiefs surrounded by pomp and display, no 'haves' and 'have-nots'. No one owned resources and benefited from that ownership as capitalists do. Instead, they found that leadership was situational. The best hunter led the hunt; the best tracker was asked to follow the spoor of a wounded animal; the women largely decided when it was time to move camp because they had to walk too far to find plant foods. Those who were seen to have the best knowledge in any sphere of life were looked up to, but only in those spheres. Situational leadership based on specialised knowledge was the accepted norm.

Today's rapidly changing world is unlikely to respond to the huge challenges it now faces by turning back the clock and resurrecting a society of hunter-gatherers like the San people! Yet countries across the globe, and churches in many different settings, may nevertheless be reminded here of the essential core of humankind – 'persons-in-relationship', each with their unique gifts to share.

This is indeed a theme emphasised repeatedly by St Paul in the letters he wrote to his young churches. He stressed that every member of Christ's body is gifted in one way or another, and that each of us has a vital part to play in the Church's ministry and mission. Initially patterns of pastoral oversight and ministry seem to have varied from place to place – small 'teams' of elders are mentioned alongside those who fulfilled specific roles (apostle, prophet, evangelist, pastor, teacher ...) – but as numbers and congregations grew, so did certain ideas, teachings and practices that led people somewhat astray. This called for more prudent supervision, and eventually to the threefold ordering of bishop, priest and deacon that has endured to this day. Yet, while universal norms are certainly necessary for the worldwide body of the Church to remain united, there must also be room for local initiatives that respond to changing circumstances, together with encouragement for 'charismatic' gifts to be expressed.

It is quite common these days in African countries for a new AIC (an 'African Initiated Church') to be born almost every week. Some of these, such as the Zionist Church in Southern Africa, have grown hugely over recent decades, while others are more localised and wither away when their founder (perhaps a dissident member of a 'mainline' church) passes away. Their variety is immense, but they usually express features of the inherited culture and respond to local needs for healing and protection, especially if there is no readily accessible 'mission' church.

In both Lesotho and Malawi it was church policy to encourage the growth of so-called 'outstations', recognising that it was unrealistic to expect Christian worshippers to make their way regularly across difficult terrain or without adequate transport to reach a main mission church (and, given that 'nature abhors a vacuum', the absence of a local place of worship is an obvious incentive for a new AIC, thus further frustrating any likelihood of unity among believers). Outstations did not, however, usually arise as a result of considered planning; rather, they developed somewhat like a plant scattering its seeds: for example, through those worshipping elsewhere discovering that they were numerous enough to gather together in their own village, where several of them then emerged as leaders. At St George's, Zomba the number of outstations grew in a relatively short time from about two dozen to nearly thirty (I was never sure of the exact figure!), each in the care of a catechist who (with suitable training) arranged for weekly services and appropriate instruction. About once a month it was possible for a priest to visit to say mass and to provide other sacraments as needed. This was also the pattern in the mountains of Lesotho, where each mission station was usually served by two priests; one would remain at the base while the other would spend a month travelling around the far-flung parish – and might stay in any particular outstation for a couple of nights, which could well be midweek rather than for a weekend. In this way, the parish retained its unity, with the scattered congregations coming together on festive occasions.

This African model of the church as a network of both larger and smaller communities has much to offer the Western church, in which at the present time, with priestly vocations rapidly declining in number, the response is all too often to close churches and to merge parishes, leaving fewer worship centres but a greater risk of anonymity (local communities being replaced by centralised crowds). This might improve the church's financial situation (less maintenance and upkeep), and also be helpful to specific areas of ministry (youth work in particular), but would it facilitate the mutual care and individual encouragement that smaller 'extended families' can more readily supply?

Given that the New Testament reminds us that 'here we have no lasting city', or in Jesus' words that 'the hour is coming when neither on this mountain nor in Jerusalem will you worship the Father', or again that in his revelation St John 'saw no temple in the (heavenly) city', there should be a certain awareness that the Church's earthly edifices, however evocative and uplifting, can only be provisional, as is true also of its institutional structures. In their forty years in the Sinai wilderness, the Israelites were after all only provided with a tabernacle (a tent) for their worship, which accompanied them on their wanderings. They were to some extent a nomadic people, like the aforementioned San bushmen – and like the Good Shepherd in his own mission and ministry! Indeed, nowhere does life stand still, and the Church needs constantly to adapt to changing situations. In such circumstances 'smallness' has the advantage of flexibility.

Although our time in Africa was limited, back in England we certainly kept African links alive. Thus, in Irchester we twinned with a mission hospital in Juba, Southern Sudan; in West Monkton with the parish of Chipili in Northern Zambia; in Sherborne with the newly created parish of Mankayane in Swaziland; in Wye with the seminary of St Charles Lwanga in Namibia. Expectations varied considerably in these far-flung locations, as it did too in both Lesotho and Malawi, but there were sometimes ways in which the 'younger' churches copied features of the 'mother' church rather too closely (forgetting the papal dictum mentioned earlier, 'The Church comes to bring Christ; she does not come to bring the culture of another race').

This was particularly noticeable in Swaziland, where I stayed with the bishop for a few nights in 2008. His hospitality was very generous, as was the time he gave in showing me around his diocese. Mbabane has a splendid cathedral, and quite a few institutions such as schools, training centres, and care homes, funded in the past through the efforts of Salesian missionaries from Italy. The bishop's problem was that hardly any Salesians remained, and their contacts with European donors had gone with them. It was extremely hard for him to maintain the extensive infrastructure they had left behind – but despite this the mission parish with which we were linked, confined to worshipping in a converted farmhouse in a rural area, still hoped that outside subsidies would give them an elaborate and very expensive European-style church of their own. The contrast with the area around Zomba in Malawi was marked: much simpler church buildings continued to spring up there – but no architects were employed, bricks were moulded and burnt locally, labour was provided free of charge, and it was only the roofing materials that needed funding from elsewhere, if at all possible. Yet 'small' was still beautiful, transformed by the fervour and commitment of those who worshipped there – as was the stable at Bethlehem by the presence of the infant Jesus (who later told us that 'whoever *humbles himself like a child*, he is the greatest in the kingdom of heaven'.)

Back in England we were taught a humbling lesson through our Zambian link. We raised money to help restore the church in Chipili, including the provision of new doors. A couple of years later, when our diocesan bishop was visiting out there, they asked him to bring back a large crucifix that had been carved especially for us, as a token of appreciation. Had we bought this through a catalogue of ecclesiastical supplies it would certainly have cost two or three thousand pounds – which was far more than they had ever received from us.

So was our whole experience in Africa: what the people did for us more than amply repaid any services rendered to them. The seven years in Africa were the best and happiest years of my life.

Deo gratias.

The light shines in the darkness, and the darkness has not overcome it. (*John 1.5*)

For it is the God who said, "Let light shine out of darkness", who has shone in our hearts to give the light of the knowledge of the glory of God in the face of Christ. (*2 Corinthians 4.6*)

www.ingramcontent.com/pod-product-compliance
Lightning Source LLC
Chambersburg PA
CBHW081827230426
43668CB00017B/2406